AF225976

BELLA ISN'T HERE ANYMORE

ANA THALLAS

Bella Isn't Here

If we can just impact one life, or one situation, then I've done something right. Then Bella's death has meaning.

—Ana Thallas

DEDICATION

To my three amazing children,

you gave me the strength to walk again.

Darian, your life has purpose, never forget that!

TABLE OF CONTENTS

PREFACE

On June 10, 2020, 21-year-old Isabella Joy Thallas (Bella) and her boyfriend Darian Simon were walking their puppy in their Denver, Colorado neighborhood. Bella was holding the leash, and stopped on a patch of grass outside an apartment building to encourage the dog to relieve himself.

The ground floor tenant on that corner, 38-year-old Michael Close, opened his window and began yelling at the couple not to let their dog defecate there. They refused. An altercation ensued. Close left, and came back with an AK-47, which he had borrowed from a Denver police officer. He opened fire.

Bella was killed almost instantly. She had her back to the window and didn't see it coming. She was shot with two rounds. Darian was a little further away and was able to run.

Meanwhile, on the other side of town, Bella's mother Ana Thallas had just finished buying a gift bag for Bella's birthday present, which she was going to give Bella when she took her out for lunch later that day. As she was about to drive away, she got a call from Bella's younger sister Lucia. She asked Ana if she had heard from Bella, saying she hadn't been able to reach her. She said there was something going on in Bella's neighborhood and that Ana should check the news.

The news was that there had been a live shooter incident in the Ballpark neighborhood where Bella had recently moved in with her boyfriend, that one victim was dead, and one was in critical condition.

They agreed to meet at the hospital. When Thallas got there, she was unable to get an answer whether her daughter was there. She realized in that moment that the victim in critical condition was Darian, which meant the one who had been killed was Bella.

The TV monitors in the waiting area were playing endless loops from the crime scene. She looked up at them and saw her daughter's tiny body covered with a tarp, a newly manicured foot sticking out the end.

When Lucia got to the hospital, the two of them drove to the crime scene. Thallas stayed there for the rest of the day. She was not permitted to go near her daughter's body or to cross the crime scene barriers, no matter how hard she begged.

In those moments the Thallas family was inducted into a not-so-uncommon nightmare in America: the death of a child to gun violence. It became a very high-profile local and regional case, which pulled Thallas into the spotlight of a media circus that didn't end until Close was sentenced 2-1/2 years later.

What follows in these pages is not the story of Bella's murder. It is not the story of the days, weeks, months, and years following. It is not the story of the investigation, the court case, the sentencing. It is not the story of the legislation. It is not the story of what Bella's siblings and friends suffered, what Ana suffered.

Ana told us she is sick of telling that story. She has told it and told it and told it, in every imaginable arena, from media, to political, to grief organizations, to private. She feels that enough is enough.

What follows in these pages is what Ana has learned as she has traveled this path. What she would like for you to know helped her. Little things to bring light into your darkness. Breadcrumbs for the journey you never asked for or dreamed you would embark on.

She offers these meditations with all the love of a grieving mother's heart, one who knows your pain regardless of what the nature of your loss is. And with her faith. And with her prayers for your healing.

Grief counsellors say the quickest way to clear a room is to tell someone you are the parent of a murdered child.

My name is Ana Thallas. I am the parent of a murdered child

SUNRISE

In the wake of any kind of catastrophic unexpected loss,

The whole world can look obscene.

It might be a beautifully sunny day,

With deep blue sky,

A few fluffy clouds scudding by above you.

How,

You wonder, could this day be so beautiful?

Without my loved one in it?

After my loved one

Has been TORN

From my arms,

By VIOLENCE

ACCIDENT,

SUICIDE,

STROKE,

You name it

Or when my home

And EVERYTHING in it,

Including all the memorabilia

of a life,

Has burned to the ground?

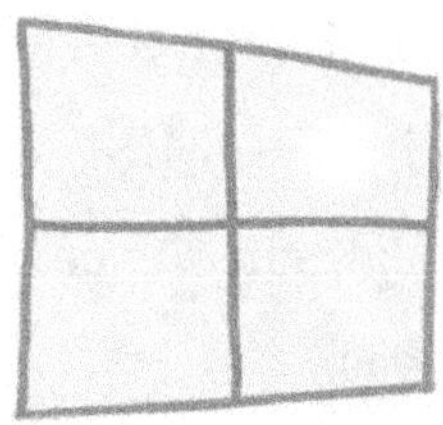

How *DARE* this day be so beautiful?!

It feels like an AFFRONT

To everything good and decent in the world.

Maybe you have been awake all night, tormented.

I have spent many tormented nights awake

Since my daughter Bella was MURDERED.

Especially in the early days, weeks, and months.

TORN

By all the images, the feelings,

THE QUESTIONS

THE REGRETS,

The unimaginable REALITY

Of her utter ABSCENCE.

Then one morning, I saw the sun rise.

Not for the first time, of course.

But this time I really *saw* it.

My eyes took in its BEAUTY.

My heart felt its PROMISE.

How the sky lightened ever so gradually.

And there it was.

The sun.

Peaking over the horizon.

Lighting up a new day.

A new sky.

Suddenly I knew that
sunrise was God's message
to me.
It doesn't matter how dark
the night is—
And you and I have lived
the darkest nights possible
in this life.
The sun always comes up.
Gloriously.
I know this sounds like a cliché.
It probably is one.
But let's not use that as an excuse
to waste its power to comfort and inspire us.
Now, whenever I see sunrise,
I hear the words of the classic hymn
"Great is Thy Faithfulness" singing inside me.

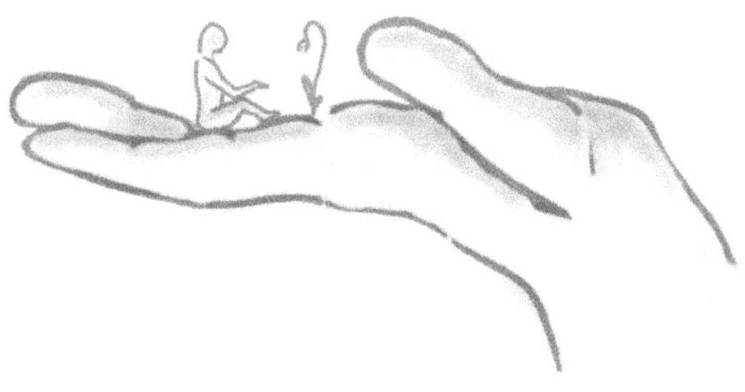

Great is thy faithfulness. Great is thy faithfulness.
Morning by morning new mercies I see.
All I have needed thy hand hath provided.
Great is thy faithfulness, Lord unto me.

It reminds me of two things:
One,
How true those words are
Two: I can live this oncoming day more peacefully,
If I look for all the evidence around me of that truth.
As you navigate the landscape
of your own unimaginable catastrophic loss,
I hope you will make it a point to get up some days before dawn
to watch the sun rise. Take in its promise of a new day.
Open your heart to the possibility it brings.

WHEN YOUR GRIEF BECOMES YOUR IDENTITY

Think with me

For a moment about how we

construct our identities.

In life,

We are so many things at

once,

Depending on the roles we

play:

Husband,

Father,

Mother,

Wife,

Companion,

Homeowner,

Business person,

Athlete…

The list goes on indefinitely.

These roles don't just create our identities,

They create our worlds.

They determine landscape within which our lives flow.

When catastrophe instantly robs us of someone

Or something inherent to who we are,

The world we knew disappears in an instant.

This is a huge shock to the body,

The soul,

The psyche.

Shock protects us a little in the first hours,

Maybe days,

But soon the devastating reality of our loss sinks in.

Or maybe better said,

We sink into the devastating reality.

Especially early on,

Our loss and our grief threatens to become who we are.

How could it not?

Maybe you went from being a new parent,

To being the bereaved parent of a baby lost to crib death.

Maybe you went from being a newlywed to a widow or
widower.

Maybe you went from being a long-time resident in a small
beach community,

To a displaced hurricane survivor.

I went from being Ana,

To being the mother of the Ballpark Murder Victim.

This is of course,

Normal,

Early on.

But you do not want to stay there.

Take it from me.

I lost myself.

In retrospect,

I see that I stayed lost for way too long.

Eventually,

I had to pull back from everything and everyone.

I had to give myself space and time to reconnect with me.

With Ana.

As you make your journey through this devastation,

Please find ways to remember who you were,

Who you still are,

And who you can become.

I know it's not easy.

I know your loss changed you,

And will continue to do so.

I also know you can determine in what direction.

Towards what outcome.

You can look for pieces of yourself,

Old and new,

Hold them up to the light,

Feel your way in to whether they fit going forward,

Find ways to incorporate them into your new self,

Your new identity,

Your new future.

ENTERTAINING ANGELS UNAWARE

In those first moments,

Of knowing that something,

Or someone you love has

been taken from you,

Everything you've always

felt you know,

All the FOUNDATIONS,

Of your UNDERSTANDING,

And EXPERIENCE

of your life FALLS AWAY.

You find yourself poking through the RUBBLE

Of your destroyed HOME,

While your neighbor's is still standing,

UNTOUCHED

The surgeon comes out to the waiting area,

And you immediately know just from the look on her face.

The policeman standing on your porch at three in the morning.

The phone call you have been dreading,

Or not even expecting at all.

That moment in the trauma center,

After I realized that Bella was the CASUALTY

Being reported,

Not the person in the operating room,

I felt an instantaneous chasm of EMPTYNESS.

For me it BURNED.

But it was also so empty.

Lucia hadn't yet arrived.

I was alone in a way I had NEVER experienced.

I was in shock.

I was devastated.

I crumpled onto a bench in the waiting area,

Sobbing,

Crying out

My daughter is dead

MY DAUGHTER IS DEAD

People were milling about.

Reporters.

Passersby.

NOBODY

Took any notice of me.

Except ONE.

ONE

Woman appeared in the crowd,

And instead of walking by,

She came right over to me.

She did not say a word.

She sat down next to me, silently.

She put her arms around

me.

And she held me as I WEPT.

In my moment of shock and

unbearable LOSS,

A STRANGER appeared,

HELD me close.

She held ME.

I don't know for how long.

I just know that the minute Lucia showed up,

She stood up and disappeared into the crowd.

I never saw her again.

Whenever I recall that moment,

The Bible's admonition,

To welcome strangers,

Because you never know when you might be

entertaining angels unaware

In the nearly three years since Bella left us,

I have learned to become AWARE,

Of when I am being held in a special way.

Sometimes moments of sudden COMFORT,

SHOW UP,

When I least expect it,

Sometimes a person shows me,

Momentary recognition and COMPASSION.

Or gives me a HUG without being asked.

I lean into those experiences.

Those

RANDOM ACTS OF KINDNESS

I receive them as the blessings they are.

I allow myself to be held.

I entertain the comfort of ANGELS.

WHY?

This is the question, isn't it?

This is the one that HAUNTS us.

That wakes us up in the middle of the night and won't let us go

back to sleep.

That no ANSWER can satisfy.

This is the heart's cry into the eternal silence that echoes back

empty.

Why did my brother end his own LIFE?

Why was my baby STILLBORN?

Why did the tornado pick MY HOUSE to land on?

Why was my BEST FRIEND walking across the street,

Just when the DRUNK DRIVER went barreling through the

intersection,

Against the red light?

The permutations are endless,

But the question is always the same:

WHY?

As a deeply spiritual person, a person of faith,

This question rocked my world from the very first moment.

How could the loving God,

I WORSHIP,

SERVE

Let this HAPPEN to my BELOVED DAUGHTER?

Not just that her life was CUT SHORT at the age of 21,

but *HOW* it was cut short.

The senselessness of it all.

I had ENTRUSTED Him with her SAFETY,

In my PRAYERS every day of her LIFE.

And now THIS?!

It is so hard to give that question up.

As humans we think in terms of cause and effect.

It helps us to have some justification,

We believe so deeply that if only we knew why,

We would not be suffering as much.

I don't know what your devastating loss was,

Or where you are in your healing journey.

But here's what I've learned on my own journey.

The question

WHY

Is a question that cannot be answered,

And even if it could, it would not satisfy you.

It won't bring you peace.

It won't fill that hole in your heart.

Because your loved one,

Like my Bella, is gone.

Nothing is going to bring them back.

That's a harsh truth, I know.

Believe me,

I know.

It takes a long time to be able to face it,

Baby steps every day,

To free you from the way,

The question

WHY

can bludgeon you when you're already down.

Eventually I came to understand,

That the God,

I was demanding answers from,

Was the same God who had created Bella.

Who had planned her life in intricate detail.

Who loves her more than I ever could have in my human-ness.

He is holding my Bella in his arms now.

Beyond the hurts of this world.

Now when the question threatens to take over my day,

I have learned to rest in my God's arms.

To take comfort there.

Where it has no more power to torment me.

My prayer for you is that you too will find a way

to release the question,

Bit by bit.

That you will find a place where your heart can rest.

THE POWER OF SURRENDER

Unexpected loss

Has a way of robbing us,

Of the feeling that we have some control in our lives.

We miscarry,

Even though we did everything in our power to have a healthy

pregnancy.

Our loved one commits suicide,

Even though we did our best to support them and lift them up.

We sandbag our home and board up the windows,

But the storm surge lifts the whole house off its foundation,

And deposits it a mile away.

Our spouse retires,

And we are looking forward to adventures,

Travels,

Visits to grandkids,

And then two weeks later,

Drops dead from a massive heart attack while making breakfast.

No matter what happens,

When it happens,

The first thing to go is our sense of control over our lives.

Powerlessness takes its place.

Ultimately,

We must learn to embrace our powerlessness,

In the face of these unthinkable events

that were beyond our control.

In the face of unimaginable loss.

Ironically, this can bring us to a new, deeper form of power.

The spiritual power of active surrender.

Of learning, bit by bit, to let go.

Bella loved butterflies.

She was in the process of starting a butterfly garden in her

apartment when she was murdered.

So at her funeral, we released butterflies.

Hundreds of them.

They all fluttered up into the sky and away.

Except for one.

It landed on Lucia's hand and

sat there as she cried.

Then it was gone.

Or so we thought.

In fact, it had flown over to

me and landed on my chest,

just above my heart.

After a while, I picked it up.

It let me pick it up and hold

it in my hand.

So calm and trusting.

When I felt ready,

I told it to be free.

It flew away.

I waited until I felt ready.

So did that butterfly.

Somehow, in the magic of that moment,

I was given an opportunity to surrender,

And relinquish some aspect of my sense of control.

At the same time, I was given another kind of power:

The opportunity to choose to release my beloved daughter in

that act of surrender.

It wouldn't be the last time I would need to choose to surrender.

But it is an image I carry in my heart,

That comes to me when things go dark.

I hope that as you walk this painful path,

You will recognize those moments of Grace,

When you can choose a deeper power than the kind you lost,

When your loved one was taken from you.

A power to receive healing and nurturing by letting go,

However momentarily.

CHANNELING HATRED
INTO POSITIVE PURPOSE

One of the most difficult aspects of grieving,

Unexpected loss,

Is the RAGE that accompanies it.

The HATE.

Hate is an

ugly word

And it's an

ugly FEELING.

But if we are to HEAL,

We must OWN it.

We must own our HATRED.

We HATE the cancer,

That caused our loved one so much SUFFERING

And then took him away from us.

We HATE the drunk driver,

Who plowed through a school crossing in the middle of the day.

We HATE the shooter,

Who mowed down our family members when they were

shopping at a mall.

We HATE the doctors who made the wrong diagnosis.

We HATE the insurance companies

who wouldn't pay for the needed treatment.

We HATE.

We HATE.

We HATE.

This hatred must be acknowledged.

It must be felt.

And it must be channeled

somehow.

For me, there was a lot to

HATE.

You can HATE the

perpetrator.

You can HATE the

system that made the

perpetrator and his

actions possible.

You can HATE the police force for failing you.

You can HATE the courts.

You can HATE the reporters.

You can even HATE God.

But here is what I learned.

If you don't channel that hatred into something positive,

It will eat you alive.

It will DESTROY you.

Ongoing hatred is the ENEMY of the human soul.

From the very beginning, I knew I had to do something.

I had to do *SOMETHING*.

And because it's just the way I am, that something had to be big.

It had to be huge.

It had to help my community HEAL.

And it had to make inroads into PREVENTING such a horror,

From happening AGAIN.

So, I WORKED with legislators to get a gun law passed.

I WORKED with the city to make a park in the middle of

Denver a memorial.

I WORKED with local people to raise funds for a basketball

court there,

And to turn Bella's murder site into a kind of sanctuary.

I know that for most of you, going big is not your thing.

And it doesn't have to be big at all,

The way you CHANNEL your hatred,

In order to transmute it to love and healing.

But my advice is to channel it into something CONCRETE.

As you sit with this meditation,

ASK yourself:

WHAT can I do?

What little thing can I do?

The answer that comes may surprise you.

And it may GROW into something that helps

HEAL THE WORLD.

At the very least, it will help HEAL you.

And that's ENOUGH.

That's MORE THAN ENOUGH.

EXERCISING DISCERNMENT

In the days

Weeks

After Bella was murdered,

I experienced a very tough lesson,

A completely unexpected lesson.

It was this:

Not everybody is going to be on your side.

Not everybody is going to be there for you.

Not everybody is going to be thinking of your needs,

Your family's needs,

As you grapple with the horrendous loss you have just suffered.

Are suffering.

This is of course particularly true,

If your loss is associated with something that gets media attention,

As mine was.

Gun violence, mass murder, catastrophic weather event.

But even if your loss was more private,

Is more private,

You will need early on to set your discernment gauge to "high."

What you need right now,

What you need going forward,

Is loving acceptance and support.

You need people who will be there for you.

People who won't use your tragedy

As an excuse to tell you all about theirs for hours on end.

People who will not subtly cast blame on you.

People who know

how to help,

Without making it seem you

owe them now.

People who can handle your

expressions of grief.

If your loss involves a media

spotlight,

People who will not use you to pursue their own agendas.

That was a huge one for me.

Finding the balance.

All that said,

You have a part to play in this.

You will have to learn,

To let go of your expectations,

About how people closer to you should be acting.

You will have to learn,

To ask for what you need,

And if it is not forthcoming,

Then you will have choices to make about that.

You will also be surprised by who does show up,

 To do the right thing,

Make your hell a little easier to bear early on.

None of this is easy.

If it's your first rodeo,

It's going to shock you.

I guess the good news is,

You will see very quickly who your true friends really are.

A lot of people cannot handle the reality of other people's

tragedies.

It's human nature.

If your child is murdered,

That means their child could be murdered.

If a brain tumor took your husband within weeks of diagnosis,

It could do the same to them.

If your baby dies of crib death,

So could theirs.

They will run in the opposite direction.

Your unexpected loss,

May not throw you into a regional media spotlight,

The way my Bella's did us.

But it will likely put you in a position,

Where you will have to tend your own garden relentlessly.

You will have to learn to discern among,

And between the people who approach you.

And when you realize,

Somebody isn't acting in what you consider your best interests,

You will have choices to make about that.

These truths may not be comforting to hear,

But not everything that helps us on this journey is comforting.

Sometimes it's a tough lesson,

That has nothing to do with being comforted.

It has to do with learning to look out for yourself,

As you navigate this new and often unbearable

passage in your life.

As you do your best to keep your own changing

needs front and center,

You will find yourself growing in ways

you never imagined possible.

WINTER WINDSHIELD BUTTERFLIES

When we open ourselves to the miraculous,

The miraculous has permission to find us.

When we are deep in the grieving process,

When the big miracle didn't come for us,

When our loved one was taken from us,

 Maybe under horrific circumstances,

We pray.

Please help me,

Please let this be a bad dream.

Please let me wake up and find them

still here with me.

No God of any kind is going to

answer our prayer.

The miracle we pray desperately for,

Won't happen.

Ultimately our job in grieving,

Is to come to terms with that cruel

truth.

Find ways to move forward.

As you know all too well,

This is not an easy task.

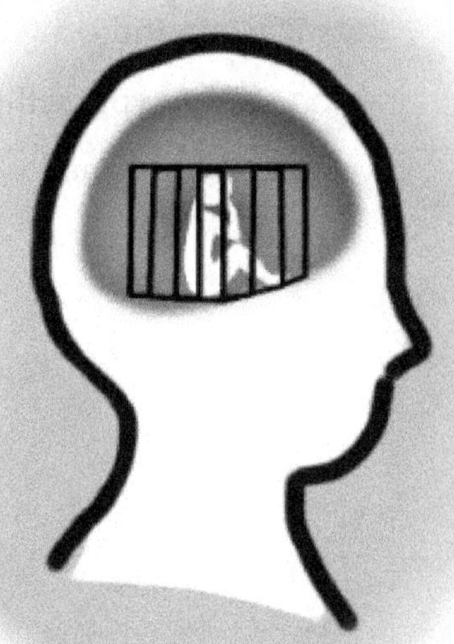

The mind is not our friend where this task is concerned.

When we are vulnerable,

Our thoughts can keep us cycling,

Around and around the drain of despair.

But smaller miracles can and do happen.

And sometimes they come,

Just when we need something,

To break the cycle of unhelpful thoughts.

That happened to me one winter day.

I was driving somewhere,

And calling some recent life decisions into question:

Was it too soon?

Am I making the right choice?

Am I still too deep in grief to do what I'm planning to do?

You know how it goes.

The vulnerability of grief can bury us in self-doubt.

I came to a stoplight.

As I sat there second-guessing myself,

A huge butterfly landed on my windshield.

In the dead of winter.

Nowhere close to butterfly season.

But there she was,

Opening and closing her wings

right in front of me.

Butterflies are a kind of talisman for me.

When I see one,

I take it as a sign that I am on the right track.

That things are going to be okay.

This one stopped that negative spiral,

Forced me to focus on something else.

Something amazing.

Something unexpected,

That shouldn't be there but was anyway.

I'd be willing to bet,

That you have experienced similar things in your journey.

Maybe it would be helpful,

To give some thought to those moments.

To remind yourself that the small miracles are there,

When you keep your eyes open for them.

ANNIVERSARIES

Loss has so many anniversaries.

Anniversaries can cut you off at the knees.

They can crush you.

No matter what caused your loss—

Car accident, suicide, aneurysm, tornado—

It is essential to find a healing approach to its anniversary.

The birthdays,

Holidays,

Dates of important milestones are all hard enough.

The hardest one,

For me anyway,

Is the anniversary of the event.

Like every choice we make when grief engulfs us,

How we approach the anniversary of the loss,

Can make or break us.

It can throw us deeper into the black hole,

Or it can help to lift us up.

It can increase our isolation,

Or it can give us the experience of community,

And show us that we are not as alone as we feel most days.

In my case,

Because of the efforts of so many in Denver

after Bella's murder,

We have a beautiful park in the heart

of the city dedicated to her.

On the anniversary of her death,

We gather together to celebrate,

To mourn,

To heal.

After sunset,

When the stars start

to shine in the night sky,

We light our candles.

We hold each other.

We sing.

We pray.

Our differences dissolve.

Our hearts and our city heal a little more.

Of course,

You don't have to create a citywide

healing event to mark your tragic loss.

Most of us don't do that.

And for many of us,

Even attending a crowded event might be too overwhelming.

Only you know what you need.

What you *can* do,

 Is make a plan to reach for some light,

As you express your grief on that day.

And to incorporate gratitude for what you had that is now gone.

Do it in whatever way has meaning for you.

Do it in the company of those who love you.

Who accept you.

Who have your back.

But do it.

THE EMPTY CHAIR

No matter how healed we get,

No matter how surrendered to our loss,

The way it has changed our lives forever,

No matter how well we are managing

to move forward with our lives,

In the aftermath,

One thing will never change.

The empty chair.

The empty chair at the

breakfast, lunch, or dinner table.

The empty seat in the living room,

When the family gathers to watch

a football game or have movie night.

The empty place around the restaurant table,

The empty seat in the movie theatre.

All those iterations of emptiness.

Because your loved one is not there anymore.

That empty chair can haunt you daily,

It can haunt you worse during family holidays,

Christmas,

Thanksgiving,

And New Year celebrations.

Early on,

I learned to fill that empty chair with thoughts of Bella.

Bella was a vivid young woman,

With lots of opinions,

And a powerful presence wherever she went.

I take comfort in imagining her reactions to things.

And sometimes I laugh out loud.

For one thing,

Right about now she'd be telling me to get over myself,

Get on with my life.

Because traveling light was her gift.

Taking life as it comes.

 Not sweating the small—

much less the big—stuff.

Maybe you can fill your empty chair too,

With memories that make you happy.

That bring your absent loved one into

the present moment with you,

Where they can encourage you.

Admonish you.

Even make you laugh.

RECONSTRUCTING THE NARRATIVE

One of the things that keeps us anchored to our loss,

Unable to move forward,

Is the retelling of our story.

Don't get me wrong.

I think it's important to tell our stories.

It's a big part of how we heal.

Early on,

It's how we convince our shocked brains that yes,

This happened.

It happened.

We have to really internalize it,

Before healing is even possible.

So we tell our story over,

And over again,

To anyone who will listen.

Including ourselves.

But there comes a point,

Where repeating the story will cripple you.

It will bury you.

And that's something I've had to battle every day.

Especially since my daughter's murder

got such a huge regional media spotlight.

It was told over,

And over again,

Especially as we hit new

milestones in the trial.

I couldn't have escaped,

Or silenced it if I had tried.

One way I've handled that,

Is to make things happen,

That help reconstruct the

narrative,

From senseless tragedy,

To things that give meaning to Bella's death.

For instance,

Early on,

We created a permanent memorial,

At the site where she was murdered.

The community paid for it with contributions,

The construction crews donated their time,

And people came,

And helped plant the butterfly garden.

It was a labor of love from beginning to completion.

And it reframed the narrative of that place.

It went from a gruesome, heart-crushing crime scene,

To a place of peace and beauty.

A place where in summer you can sit in the sun on a bench,

With your bare feet on warm grass,

Surrounded by flowering plants

that attract butterflies and other pollinators.

Sitting there,

You can let the beauty and comfort of this space

shape your thoughts.

They can become thoughts of replenishment and rejuvenation.

Thoughts of how the cycles of life keep going,

Of how good things still happen in this world.

I wonder how you might be able to replicate

something like this in your life?

How many times have you told the story?

Is it time to change the narrative?

To add something new?

Some hope?

Something that restores your faith in your God

- if you have one,

In yourself,

And in the world?

WHEN GRIEF OVERWHELMS US

Sometimes no matter what we do,

The grief comes in,

Like a tsunami,

And sweeps away all our self-care,

Healing practices,

Erasing what we may think

of as our progress,

In moving forward.

Grief is unpredictable that way.

It comes in waves,

But it doesn't warn us.

It comes,

And then we are drowning.

There is no air to come up for.

That happens to me when I dream of Bella.

I dream of her as a small child.

When I wake up, I can feel her little arms around me.

How soft her skin was.

The scent of her, the texture of her hair.

The warmth of her body.

Her little heart beating against my chest when we snuggled.

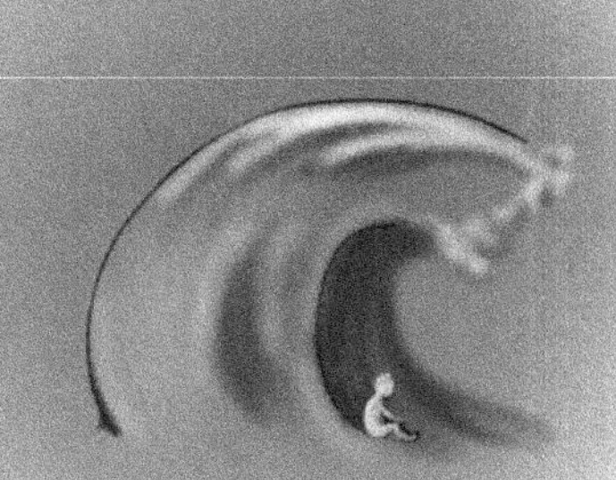

All the most visceral, embodied memories of the child I loved.

These dreams crush me.

I imagine that for you, it may be similar.

Maybe not a dream, but maybe a memory.

Or driving by a place you used to go.

Or seeing a picture.

Somebody else walking down the street,

With a baby strapped to her back,

Who is the same age as the one you lost to crib death.

A pregnant woman.

A happy couple.

People playing with their kids in the park.

And suddenly there it is,

Swallowing you whole.

Your consciousness of your deep loss.

Your emptiness.

It is so important that you learn not to stay there.

Yes, feel your feelings.

Give yourself a little time,

A little space,

To let the grief move through you,

Like the wave that it is.

But sooner or later,

You'll need to rise up

Take action that will help you move off that dime.

The action I take on days like that,

Is to go to Bella's grave.

I stay there as long as I need to.

I feel what I feel.

I cry.

I give in to the pain.

One such day,

It was so bad,

All I could do was lie,

Belly down on the earth that covers her,

Soaking the ground with my tears.

Somehow,

I fell asleep.

I slept for several hours.

When I woke up,

I was surrounded by a family of deer.

Grazing peacefully all around me.

I have never seen so many deer in one place,

Certainly none who exhibited no fear of the human nearby.

For a while I just lay there,

Not wanting to frighten them away.

I felt so comforted by the gentleness emanating from them.

The peace in their presence.

Finally, I sat up.

I was half expecting the deer to bound away,

But they didn't.

They looked up.

Some turned their heads towards me.

A few made eye contact.

That was it.

They just kept on grazing.

And filling my heart with a deep peace.

That's the thing, isn't it?

Even when we are most at the mercy of our grief,

The Divine orchestrates something—

No matter how small—

To remind us:

You are not alone.

In order to have access to such a moment,

We must be in motion ourselves.

We must take a step forward to meet it.

To make space for it.

May you gather the courage,

The self-love to take whatever action feels most right to you,

When you need to step out of the grief.

I know these moments of Divine Grace

will meet you more than halfway.

They will come for you as they have for me.

And I encourage you to be open to them.

Notice them.

And take them to heart.

TINY MESSENGERS

In the aftermath of catastrophic loss,

Some events can radically challenge our healing progress,

Our sense of our own strength to handle what comes,

Our budding and oh-so-fragile trust in the goodness of life,

That is beginning to re-emerge.

It can be anything, really.

Small or LARGE.

The hospital bill arrives for the care

that didn't save your loved one.

A happy vacation postcard arrives,

After your loved one died of a stroke on a luxury cruise.

Or for some of you,

A court case.

For me,

It was a particular part of the prosecution of Bella's murderer.

Evidence to assess the degree of GUILT

was going to be presented.

We had the CHOICE not to be present in the courtroom.

As Bella's MOTHER,

I felt a deep need to WITNESS,

To experience the MOMENT, she left her body.

I thought it would give me some kind of CLOSURE.

That I would *KNOW* it on a deeper level of my being.

I thought I was PREPARED.

I was NOT prepared.

Those images,

They BROKE me.

We went to her park afterwards.

I sat on the bench DEDICATED to her,

SOBBED.

A tiny ladybug landed on my hand.

She sat there on my finger the entire time as I WEPT.

When I was all cried out, and READY,

I told her

"It's time for you to fly and be FREE."

I lifted my hand.

She flew off.

I felt in that moment,

It was Bella,

Saying to me

"IT'S OKAY, MAMA.

You can let me go. It's time to let me go now.

It's time to live your life."

Your worldview may not include the idea,

That your passed-on loved ones can be present with you.

That's okay.

But GRIEF has a way of softening us,

Of OPENING our perceptions in new ways.

We can FIGHT it;

We can armor up,

As a SURVIVAL strategy.

I think that would be a MISTAKE.

If you let your grief soften you,

You give the natural world the OPPORTUNITY

To send you these tiny messengers of COMFORT,

In a way that has MEANING for you.

BELIEVE ME,

They will come.

FACING THE EMPTINESS INSIDE

When you lose a loved one SUDDENLY,

A CHASM OF EMPTINESS

OPENS up inside you.

You may not notice it early on.

You're in SHOCK.

You're in DENIAL.

You have all those details to manage:

The funeral,

The calls and visits,

and in my case,

The media and the murder investigation.

At some point though,

The emptiness SETS IN.

Or rather, you NOTICE it.

And then you CAN'T un-notice it.

I know your lost loved one is always in the back of your mind.

Like you,

I find myself thinking,

"Oh, I need to call Bella,"

And then realize AGAIN,

That BELLA ISN'T THERE.

Or I hear the door to the house open.

I EXPECT to see Bella.

But it isn't Bella,

It NEVER will be again.

These CONSTANT daily experiences,

DRIVE home to you,

That your loved one is GONE forever.

And your emptiness DEEPENS with each realization.

I'm not sure there's a SOLUTION to that.

Like anything in the grieving process,

It's something that ebbs and flows even as a CONSTANT.

 Because NOTHING will ever fill that particular emptiness.

So we have to find a way to *USE* it.

You will simply have to FIND a reason to GO ON.

You will have to find YOUR own reason.

Maybe several reasons.

A big one for ME is my two remaining children.

They need me to be PRESENT

with them and for them.

They NEED me to get up

in the morning.

They keep ME going,

Even on the WORST of days.

And so I DO.

I KEEP going.

I keep HEALING.

What is YOUR reason to go on?

If you don't know,

WHO can you talk with,

WHO will help you figure it out?

Your emptiness is NOT all there is to your life,

Even if it feels like it is.

There is MORE to you than this.

You too have VALUE.

SOMEBODY

Or SOMETHING needs you.

FIND THEM.

And KEEP going.

MANAGING ISOLATION

GRIEF can be very isolating.

It's our NATURAL impulse,

To HIDE away from the outside world,

When we're in overwhelming emotional PAIN.

Everything is so RAW.

Your nervous system is on FIRE.

Your world has COLLAPSED around you

It feels DAUNTING just to get to the grocery store.

You'll have BETTER days and WORSE days.

If you're an outgoing person,

You may not have trouble getting yourself out there enough,

To maintain some BALANCE and perspective—

And, to be honest—some much needed DISTRACTION.

If you're more of an introvert,

You're going to have to really STAY

on top of the tendency to hide away.

When we're alone a lot,

It's EASY for our thoughts,

MEMORIES,

REGRETS,

WHAT-IFS,

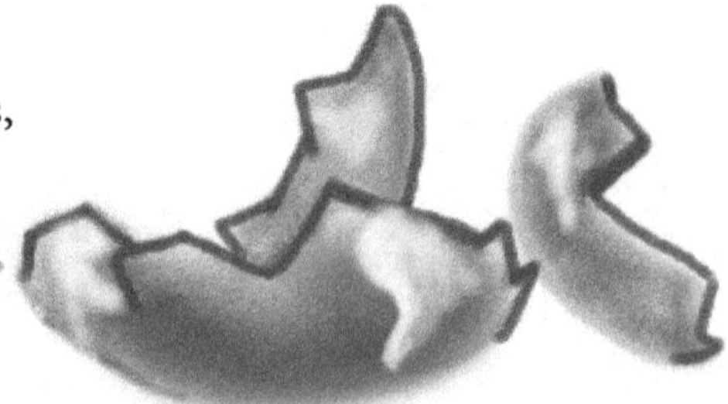

To lead us down a rabbit hole to DESPAIR.

I think it's also IMPORTANT,

Not to believe your thoughts,

If they tend to LEAD you to hunker down at home all the time.

SOMETIMES it's worth a shot to accept an invitation.

No matter what YOUR thoughts tell you.

Or to MAKE an invitation.

To FORCE yourself to take a shower,

Get dressed in something

that makes you feel GOOD about yourself,

VENTURE out into the world,

So it can SHOW you its good side (it has one).

Or have SOMEBODY over,

To EXPERIENCE the healing camaraderie

that happens in good company.

WHO or WHAT comes to mind as you read this?

Maybe start THERE.

I think YOU will be glad you did.

A COMMUNITY OF GRIEF

One of the most important things you can do,

As you walk the path of healing,

From seemingly insurmountable loss

Is to connect with a community of grief.

The most obvious community,

Of course,

Is a grief group.

Where you will be able to sit with other bereaved people at

different stages of healing

and learn from them.

Teach them.

Within the guidance of an experienced counsellor.

The healing power of a well-led grief group can't be overstated.

But it also might not be enough.

It certainly wasn't for me.

If anything,

It's a jumping off place.

I am an action-oriented person.

I have to be able to take action,

To see the fruits of my labors.

The more concrete the better.

Looking back,

I realize now

That most of my efforts in the community after Bella's murder

Were about creating spaces where grieving people could gather,

Informally,

And in any size group.

I see these gathering spots as places,

Where a community of grief can come and find relief.

A community can be just you and a friend,

Or your family,

Or a group of people who knew and loved your lost one.

There's no right way.

This community of grief will ebb and flow over time

As the seasons of healing pass.

Where you meet can be anywhere.

You don't have to be like me

And spearhead a community effort

to build spaces in your town for it.

You can meet at your church.

A hiking trail.

A coffee shop.

Make it what works for you.

Just please be sure to stay connected to your world.

Make space for you to give and receive love and understanding

Within your community of grief.

Nobody else can understand you the way they can.

And right now you need understanding

more than you ever may have.

So you can heal.

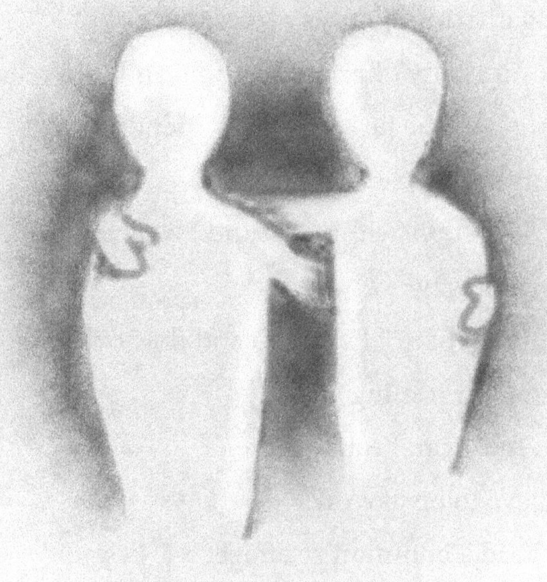

MOVING ON OR MOVING FORWARD?

People say the goal with mourning is to move on.

I disagree.

Maybe it's just semantics.

But this is something I feel strongly about.

You don't have to leave behind whatever

Or whomever you have lost,

Your lost future on a timeline where they were present.

You don't have to practice seeing them get smaller,

And smaller in the rearview mirror of your life.

Grief isn't linear,

Neither is healing.

They were real.

They were important.

They mattered.

They still do.

They always will.

You can take them with you.

In whatever way makes sense to you.

Helps you.

That will probably look different as your healing progresses.

It's up to you how it looks.

It's your loss.

It's your healing.

You get to define what that looks like.

Taking charge of it in that way,

Will empower you in a process,

That feels from the get-go to be utterly disempowering.

As for me?

I will never move on.

I will move forward,

And that is something I work on every day.

But my Bella is in my heart.

Bella is my heart.

I will mourn her every day of my life.

I will celebrate her.

I will not move on from Bella.

I will carry her with me.

Cherish her as she deserves to be cherished.

And in so doing I will have the richest healing I could wish for.

How might you envision a healing that includes your lost one(s)?

What kind of a future would that be for you?

How might you make moving forward,

A way to embrace them even in their absence,

While embarking on this new landscape ahead,

In a way that brings you happiness,

Satisfaction,

Joy?

GRIEF AND GRATITUDE

Here's something that really surprised me.

In a good way.

Even in the midst of the worst loss I could possibly imagine,

Even so deep in grief sometimes I couldn't get out of bed,

There was always,

Always something to be grateful for.

And the more I saw what there was to be grateful for,

The more I saw…

What there was to be grateful for.

After a while it seemed to me that grief and gratitude are two sides of the same coin.

For example, I am still grateful that my daughter did not suffer.

She did not see the AK-47 sticking out the ground floor window.

She was engaging with her puppy.

She had no fear.

With 24 rounds, she was killed instantly.

That may seem an odd thing to be grateful for,

Given how horrendous it is,

But there it is.

I am grateful for it.

I am not suggesting to you that you look

for pat little ways to downplay your loss.

Or even that you do something like write

a gratitude list each day

(although that can actually be a very comforting,

Soothing and eye-opening thing to do!).

Or that the good things that happen,

In the context of your grief

By any stretch of the imagination trivialize it.

I am suggesting that you stay open

to seeing both sides of the coin.

Open out your perspective.

See what treasures it brings you.

SUNSET

When we are healing from devastating sudden LOSS,

Our days can seem ENDLESS.

They can seem INSURMOUNTABLE.

Sometimes they *are* insurmountable and on THOSE days we go

back to bed.

Justifiably so.

But most of us have RESPONSIBILITIES

we have to step up to.

People who NEED us.

Employers or clients EXPECTING us,

To SHOW UP,

To DELIVER.

Meals to get on the table for FAMILIES.

Bills to PAY.

KIDS to deliver to school and activities.

All the minutiae of daily life that doesn't GO AWAY,

Even though our loved one is NOT THERE anymore.

Because these activities are so MUNDANE—

We did them without even THINKING about it,

BEFORE we found our lifeless baby in the crib,

Or the phone call CAME,

Or the tsunami HIT—

We take it for GRANTED that we should be able to do them.

That we don't deserve any REWARD for getting through a day.

After all, it's just a DAY.

EVERYBODY does it.

Well, it actually isn't JUST a day.

The way it USED to be.

The way it is for those who are going about their LIVES,

With their homes INTACT

And their loved ones AROUND.

Not for US it isn't.

Getting THROUGH a day can be a major accomplishment.

Not EVERY day.

And as we HEAL,

Fewer and FEWER in a week or month.

But still.

I like sunset.

Sunset REMINDS me that

God in His mercy and Wisdom

Has given us MARKERS to measure our days with.

And sunset means:

Job WELL done.

You MADE IT through the day.

I'm going to suggest you do a little experiment.

Just for the next week or so,

Find a way to SIT with the sunset.

Let its truth SINK in:

I DID IT.

I MADE IT THROUGH.

BASK in the beauty that is always available to you,

Always CHANGING.

And let it COMFORT you

THE EYE OF THE STORM

A point comes in all of this when you bottom out.

When you've seen all you need to see,

To really get that your loved one is gone.

Or your home.

Or whatever it is that has suddenly disappeared.

You're no longer in denial.

You're no longer bargaining with God.

The maelstrom may still be raging around you.

Even inside you.

But you find a place,

Right in the center of all that.

The eye of the storm.

It's calm there.

You are calm there.

You look around and you are safe.

You see that you are not the storm,

The storm is not you.

You see that nothing you could have done

Would have stopped what happened from happening.

You see that there's no use for blame,

For guilt,

For regret,

For shame.

What you had is gone.

It's gone now and it is not coming back.

You accept that fact.

You sit down on the ground in the eye of the storm and let

acceptance come.

Not for long, maybe.

Not for even five minutes.

But once you have done that,

You will learn to do it again.

And again.

And again.

You will learn that you have a refuge on the inside.

If you have a God,

You will stay there as long as you can with your God.

If you don't,

You will still find your peace there.

I promise.

Find the eye of

the storm whenever you can.

Learn to sit there in

the deep peace

of acceptance.

JUST LOOK UP

It's amazing what we can see,

When we open our eyes to the beauty around us.

If you're like me,

You'll take those moments,

To mean that your loved one is watching over you from heaven.

Or your God is.

Regardless,

You can still find comfort,

In the beauty of the world you are walking through,

So bereft.

Especially on difficult days,

I like to look up.

Into the sky.

Towards the sun.

When I do that with my sunglasses on,

I sometimes see a kind of rainbow figure in the clouds.

It's always the same shape.

The colors shimmer.

It always makes me feel so much better.

Protected, somehow.

Encouraged.

Feeling I can go on.

There's a scientific explanation for such images in the clouds,

I am told.

To be honest,

I couldn't care less what the scientific reason is.

I don't know if my mind is constructing the image out of a

psychological need,

Or if the image is somehow,

Truly there in the outside world,

Because of how light refracts through water.

Whatever.

I don't need to know what it's made of.

I don't need it explained away.

What I need is to see it.

I look up, and the rainbow figure in the clouds is there.

Whenever I need it to be.

That makes all the difference to me.

I wonder what you might see when you look up.

I hope you try it.

DIAMONDS IN THE SKY

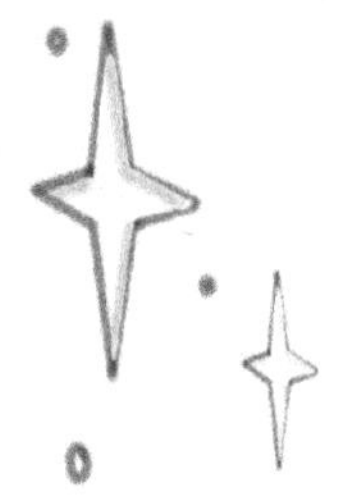

If you just lie quietly

in the grass at night

if you are truly still

allow yourself to feel

the earth breathe

under you

through you

you can *feel* it

you see the stars for what they are

you see the moon for what it is

your grief leaves you

for one minute

for two minutes

because you can see

the diamonds in the sky

how they sparklea

and you know

she

is one of them

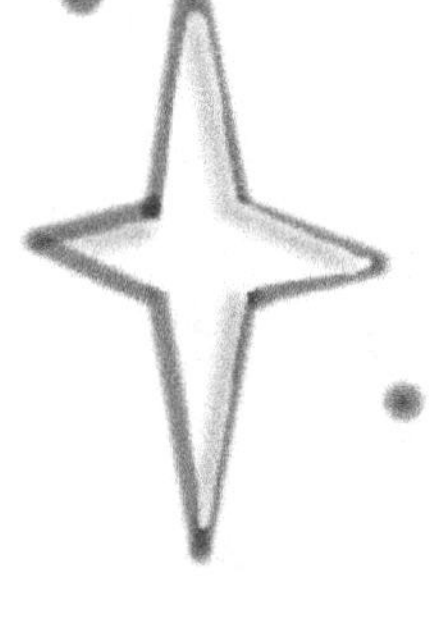

EPILOGUE

At what point do we forgive?

Do we have to forgive?

Do we want to forgive is the bigger question.

As soon as I left the sentencing for Bella's murderer I was bombarded with calls, texts, emails, etc.

One still haunts me. I was told that it was obvious I was bitter and hopefully I can move on now.

Not only did that break my heart even more but it made me mad. It hurt.

Now I'm being perceived as a bitter woman because my daughter is dead.

My victim impact statement was ruined because the Judge refused to allow me to look, speak or even glance in his direction.

My words were fumbled by the burning sensation in my heart. I couldn't focus, I couldn't breathe.

Isabella was slaughtered in broad daylight but I must portray a perfect Christian woman.

No!

As a believer we are called to forgive as Christ forgave us. His words on the cross, "Forgive them for they know not what they do."

But when?

When all of this happened, as it unfolded, as my life was picked apart, piece by piece, I felt an overwhelming sense of the need to be perfect. Look perfect, my children dressed perfectly, address the courts with manners, wear appropriate clothing for all interviews. Make it appear as though grief is easy, somewhat glamorous.

Absolutely not!

Bitter, you bet! Hurt, still cry weekly if not daily, absolutely! Bella is dead.

I move forward, I look for those small things we shared, I must find something to pull myself out of despair. I listen to a lot of classical music now, Christian music when I Pray and throughout the day, Bella's music to get my day going.

It's those things that refocus me. Then I can address my bitterness, broken heart, anxiety and depression.

Music has lead me through so many difficult moments in life and beautiful memories that I will never forget.

As I sat through the murder trial, I wore one AirPod with songs that bring me comfort. Watching the videos of the incident, coroner reports (24 pages of Bella's body) listening to Darian speak his truth of being gunned down…. I'm melting inside, my head is throbbing, I didn't eat all week or sleep. Keep in mind you are being watched by the media at all times, the murderers family and of course my children.

Focus Ana, focus on the melody, the harmony, the beauty. This too shall pass…

Give yourself grace. Don't force your forgiveness, don't make yourself do something you're not ready to do.

It's between you and God.

No one knows your true journey, no one can walk it.

As time goes on the pain is constant but you have something to look forward to. A brighter day, a beautiful song, a sunset melody.

www.ingramcontent.com/pod-product-compliance
Lightning Source LLC
Chambersburg PA
CBHW070728030726
47601CB00002B/181